Devotions for
Mothers

Hester M. Monsma, Compiler

BAKER BOOK HOUSE
Grand Rapids, Michigan 49506

The Revised Standard Version is used for all Scripture texts.

This material is taken from the *Daily Manna* Series, for many years edited by the late Dr. Martin Monsma and by his son, Dr. Tim Monsma, after his father's death in 1968. The authors of the devotions in this booklet are:

Henry Baker 26; William P. Brink 18; John De Jong 8; John C. De Korne 12, 16; Sidney De Waal 22; Harry A. Dykstra 13; Henry J. Evenhouse 23; E. Furda 9; Leonard Greenway 20; Jake Heerema 28; E. Raymond Hemphill 24; F. M. Huizenga 11, 27; J. B. Hulst 1; William Kok 7; John H. Primus 10; William K. Stob 30; William A. Swets 15; J. Vander Ploeg 14; F. Vander Stoep 25; Seymour Van Dyken 17, 19; Rolf L. Veenstra 5; N. L. Veltman 29; John C. Verbrugge 2, 3; Simon Viss 21; N. Vogelzang 6; C. Witt 4.

Copyright 1984 by
Baker Book House Company

ISBN: 0-8010-2942-2

Printed in the United States of America

1 They Labor in Vain

Bible Reading: Psalm 127

Unless the Lord builds the house, those who build it labor in vain   Ps. 127:1a.

Having read this part of the Bible, pause just a moment and look around.

Now what do you see? Probably you have seen a well-built house, equipped with all the comforts and mechanical conveniences of our age. There is also your husband, your sons, or daughters. You've seen everything that is necessary for a happy and successful home.

But the writer of this Psalm states that these elements are not enough. You may possess everything necessary for a happy home, but, "Unless the Lord builds the house, those who build it labor in vain."

The psalmist does not mean that we can sit idly by, looking to God for that which is necessary to provide us with a readymade home and family. But while we plan and work we must realize that apart from His grace and blessing, we plan and work in vain. Only when home-builders look to God and depend on His covenantal grace as revealed in Christ, can they be assured that they have everything necessary for a happy and successful household.

2 Her Children Call Her Blessed

Bible Reading: Proverbs 31:10–31

Her children rise up and call her blessed; her husband also, and he praises her Prov. 31:28.

What an indescribable blessing when the mother in a home answers to the description of a virtuous woman given in this chapter. Happy that husband who has received her. Happy, too, those children who may grow up under her care. What a boon it would be to the society of our day if the majority of homes could claim to be so favored.

Children often do not appreciate their mother until they have left home to establish their own home. Children can be so thoughtless. They do not notice the unwearied devotion, the self-sacrificing love, and the prayerful concern which mother bestows on them. Their eyes are opened when they leave home. When the daughter becomes a mother herself, she begins to understand. When a son leaves home and the cold blasts of human heartlessness blow squarely into his face, the tender care and the self-denying love of his mother suddenly stand out in bold relief.

A husband, too, all too often, takes for granted the endless service performed by the mother of his children in the home. How long a faithful wife and diligent mother must sometimes wait for that word of praise and encouragement which might make her burden lighter and put a new song into her heart. If it is true that a mother's work is never finished, then the labors of those diligent hands ought not to be unnoticed.

3 Birth

Bible Reading: 1 Samuel 1:12– 20

. . . there is . . . a time to be born. Eccles. 3:2a.
For this child I prayed 1 Sam. 1:27a.
Thou didst knit me together in my mother's womb Ps. 139:13b.

Wonder and mystery surround the birth of a child. Children are always fascinated when a new baby comes into the home. Thousands of children are born into the world every day. Man is learning much about the hidden process of conception. Yet the wonder and the mystery remains.

In the womb of the mother, unseen by human eyes, life is formed. The body in all of its amazing complexity is taking shape, every part imbedded marvelously in the germ of the tiny beginning. And in some mysterious way the factors that will shape the mind and the personality of the new-formed life, are being woven into that living organism.

How far humanity has strayed from due reverence for life, and due reverence for the God of life, when they say that a pregnant woman has the right to do with her body what she wants to do, and then lay bloody hands on the life conceived in her womb.

When Hannah had given birth to her son, she called him Samuel, saying, "I have asked him of the Lord," and her testimony to Eli was, "For this child I prayed." Her heart was filled with praise as she thought on the wonder of God's grace and power in her conception.

Parents of a newborn infant, join hands with Hannah. Join with her in praising the God of life.

4 What Have They Seen in Your House?

Bible Reading: 2 Kings 20:12–19

He said, "What have they seen in your house?" 2 Kings 20:15.

King Hezekiah had almost died. Miraculously he had been restored again and had the joy of knowing that another fifteen years would be added to his life. His unusual experience became known even in the land of Babylon and the king made use of it as an excuse for doing a bit of spying. Messengers were sent supposedly to congratulate Hezekiah on his good fortune. They kept their eyes wide open, and after returning to their master, told him much about the strength of Judah.

Shortly afterward Isaiah came to Hezekiah and put to him the question of our text. When Hezekiah admitted that he had shown the messengers everything that was in his house, the prophet reprimanded him for having done a foolish thing.

What do people see in your house? Do they feel they are in a Christian home when they visit you? Is that fact evident not only from a plaque hanging on the wall, but also from the way in which things are managed in your home? The training of children begins in the home. Deep impressions are made on them early in life. If our homes are under the sway of Christ, are places where the Bible is held in reverence and where conduct is consciously modeled after God's will, we need not fear greatly for the future of our children. What's in your house? Do the books, music, and the conversation in your house proclaim a Christian home?

5 All Things Are Yours

Bible Reading: 1 Corinthians 3:16– 23

*For all things are yours . . . and you are
Christ's*   1 Cor. 3:21, 23.

When I look at the food I am eating, I often
wonder just how many people were involved in pro-
ducing, packaging, and delivering it for me and my
family to enjoy. It takes hundreds of people to bring
the bread to my table, or the coffee from South America. And the same is true of clothes, TV, or car.

Then think how many more people are involved in
your salvation! Think how many people God uses in
order to bring your soul to heaven! I do not mean
simply your parents, your Sunday-school teachers, and
the ministers whom you have heard. Think of the many
men who wrote the Bible, and all the people about
whom they wrote. Paul says that things happened to
them for *our* example and admonition!

Hundreds of people are needed to compose and print
hymns and to build churches. In fact, you can almost
say that the Holy Spirit uses the entire world to save
your soul. Isn't it wonderful?

And what are you doing as your share in that wide-
spread work? Are you helping the kingdom of Heaven
at all by being in the world? Are you merely a parasite
who takes all and gives nothing? Are you a help or a
hindrance to other Christians?

6 In the Kitchen

Bible Reading: Zechariah 14:1– 5; 16– 21

And on that day there shall be inscribed on the bells of the horses "Holy to the Lord" . . . and every pot in Jerusalem and Judah shall be sacred to the Lord of hosts. Zech. 14:20, 21.

Holy to the Lord!

Is that what you say of your work in the kitchen? Not only will you say it on that great day of the Lord but you must learn to say it and experience it every day in your work-a-day world among the pots and pans.

A young woman, one of eight children in a busy household, had gone on Christian volunteer work. She had worked hard during those six weeks of summer teaching children the Bible, supervising the crafts in Vacation Bible School, and giving evangelistic talks to various groups. She came home aglow from her mountaintop experience. Throwing her suitcase on her bed she said with arms flung wide "Oh, Mother, don't you wish you could have been working for the Lord this summer?" The mother, wan and tired, discreetly said "I have my daughter—I have—only in a little different way."

Do you have that daily awareness, mother, that your calling is just as holy as the pastor's? And that "Holy to the Lord" must not only be written on the pulpit but also on the cupboard shelves and on the kitchen stove?

7 Parents and Children

Bible Reading: Proverbs 1:8–19

*Hear, my son, your father's instruction, and
reject not your mother's teaching* Prov. 1:8.

In these words we have an admonition to children
to honor their father and mother. Undoubtedly this
admonition was necessary when Solomon wrote these
words. Every generation it has been necessary to remind children of their obligation to their parents. The
sinful heart is a rebellious heart. One of the most difficult things to learn is obedience to authority. In our
day, too, it is necessary to remind the children that
they must heed the instruction of their fathers and not
forsake the law of their mothers.

But fathers and mothers should realize that the words
of our text place a tremendous responsibility on them.
Fathers must be sure that their instruction is true and
right; and mothers must see to it that the law which
they present to their sons and daughters is in harmony
with the law of God.

God makes fathers and mothers the counselors of
their children. Children must listen to their parents and
submit themselves. It becomes a serious consideration
for the parents whether or not they are trustworthy
guides. Can you honestly say to your children, "Look
at us and follow in our steps"?

Fathers and mothers love their children; but our love
for them is no guarantee that we will lead our children
in the way in which they ought to go. Constantly search
your hearts and their lives so that their guidance meets
with the approval of the Lord. Children sin when they
do not heed the instruction of father and mother. But
parents sin when they are not living examples of holi-
ness and devotion.

8 Ruth — The Gleaner

Bible Reading: Ruth 2:14– 23

So she gleaned in the field . . . then she beat out what she had gleaned, and it was about an ephah of barley Ruth 2:17.

Ruth as a gleaner teaches us a significant lesson in economics and sociology. The account extols the great virtue of thrift. The family of Naomi went to Moab for economic reasons and was sadly disillusioned. Ruth then gladly took advantage of the privileges which Israel's law afforded her to assist Naomi by providing a living for her. Nothing was too humble for Ruth, if it was honorable. Many people in Old Testament times considered work to be degrading.

Scripture exalts labor. However, in the laws God gave Israel are provisions which allow the poor to provide for their livelihood. The law of gleaning is an example. Harvesters in Israel were not to look too closely for all the grain which the harvest yielded but were to leave some grain for the poor. The poor must, however, glean the grain; in other words, they must work for it.

Jesus also gives us an important lesson in thrift. After He had fed thousands with a few loaves and fishes, He commanded His disciples to gather the fragments so that nothing would be lost. What a lesson for wasteful America! When godliness, which is profitable unto all things, leaves us, the virtue of thrift also passes by the board. Ruth, the godly one, is also an excellent example of thrift.

9 Rich in Mercy

Bible Reading: Ephesians 2:1—10

But God, who is rich in mercy, out of the great love with which he loved us, even when we were dead through our trespasses, made us alive together with Christ (by grace you have been saved) Eph. 2:4—5.

A mother asked Napoleon to pardon her son. The emperor said that it was his second offense, and justice demanded his death. "I don't ask for justice," said the mother, "I plead for mercy." "But," said the emperor, "he does not deserve mercy." "Sire," cried the mother, "it would not be mercy if he deserved it, and mercy is all I ask for." "Well then," said Napoleon, "I will have mercy." And her son was saved.

We have to do with One, far greater than Napoleon, namely God, who is rich in mercy. Praise His holy name! We do not deserve mercy—we need not deserve it, for He loved us first! He looked down from heaven and saw us helpless and hopeless, but His love planned the way of salvation.

Our God is plenteous in mercy, and His Word speaks often of the greatness and of the multitude of mercy that endures forever. It is all of mercy! Is there any room then for boasting? None whatsoever! "By grace you have been saved."

> Marvelous grace of our loving Lord,
> Grace that exceeds our sin and our guilt,
> Yonder on Calvary's mount outpoured,
> There's where the blood of the Lamb was spilt.
> Marvelous grace, infinite grace
> Grace that is greater than all our sin.

10 Loving Laws

Bible Reading: Exodus 20:1–6

I am the Lord your God, who brought you out of the land of Egypt, out of the house of bondage Exod. 20:2.

Our teenage daughter challenged us the other day. "That's a dumb rule!" she muttered in reaction to some restriction we placed on her. We tried to explain, but it is often hard to give a good, reasonable argument for parentally made rules. Somehow we have to show that the rules are for our children's own good; we make rules for them because we love them.

That's the way God did it. He gave ten rules to His children, the Israelites, but He made it clear that He was making rules not to bind them but to free them; not to make life miserable but to make it happy. The Ten Commandments were given in a context of grace and love. "I am the Lord your God, who brought you out of the land of Egypt, out of the house of bondage." Those are words of love, because they call to mind the great redemptive event of the Old Testament—the exodus out of Egypt. Only after reminding them of His great love, did God give His children the rules. It is as though He is saying, "Look, I love you so much I freed you from bondage. Now if you want to remain free, do this, and this, and this. Above all, serve and worship the true and living God alone. If you do, you will have joy, happiness, and freedom. If you don't, you will go back into bondage again—the bondage of sin."

Good rules, good laws, are precious things. For they are means of grace, love, and freedom. No wonder the Israelites sang, "Oh, how love I Thy law!"

11 A Parent's Concern

Bible Reading: Genesis 27:41—28:5

*And Rebekah said to Isaac . . . if Jacob marries
one of the Hittite women . . . what good will
my life be to me? Then Isaac called Jacob . . .
and charged him, You shall not marry one of
the Canaanite women* Gen. 27:46; 28:1.

Would that all parents today had Rebekah's
earnest concern about the marriage of their sons and
daughters! Rebekah considered that a marriage of her
son, Jacob, to one of the unbelieving girls of the Hit-
tites would be a tragedy of the greatest magnitude in
her life. She felt that if Jacob should enter into such a
union, life for her would hardly be worth living.

Rebekah had a clear understanding of the tremendous and far-reaching importance of marriage. She
understood, too, how absolutely essential religious unity
and agreement are to true marital happiness. She dis-
cerned accurately what grave tragedy and frightful danger are involved when a believer marries one who does
not share his or her faith.

If parents saw this as clearly as Rebekah did, they
would do all they could to forestall and prevent such
tragic and sinful unions. They would not be content to
simply say that marriage is the affair only of the son
or the daughter, and parents must observe a strict
"hands off" policy. Christian parents will not be ready
to assume that every "nice" girl is a Christian girl and
a suitable partner for their son; and will do all possible
to help and lead their son or daughter to a truly God-
pleasing marriage.

12 The Home and the Mission Field

Bible Reading: Mark 16:14–20

When you sit in your house Deut. 6:7.
Go into all the world and preach the gospel to the whole creation Mark 16:15.

The home can be the mission field's best friend; it can also be its greatest enemy, depending on the point of view. That statement needs a word of explanation.

Christian homes have been the Church's best nurseries for missionary recruits. In the home the growing child gathers deep convictions. Homes in which parents speak with appreciation for the missionary enterprise of the Church are the homes that will produce the missionaries of the next generation. Many a missionary has traced the first stirrings of missionary ambitions to the conversations heard at the family table. Christian missionaries usually come from Christian homes.

The home, by a perverse use of its appeal, has often been the enemy of the missionary enterprise. Many young men and women of high Christian ideals were ready to do anything for their Lord—except to leave home! Some young adults who have been leaders of missionary promotion in their own churches have refused to give serious consideration to a missionary call—because it would take them so far away from their relatives!

The home is a precious heritage; God hath set the solitary in families. But God is first. "He who loves father or mother more than me is not worthy of me." "He who loses his life for my sake will find it."

13 We Must All Appear

Bible Reading: 2 Corinthians 5:1–10

For we must all appear before the judgment seat of Christ   2 Cor. 5:10a.

The greatest certainty concerning the length of our days is the uncertainty. A visit to one of our crowded hospitals will convince one of that. There is also startling suddenness in the death of those who are victims of our modern tragedies. A gracious God labors to impress this uncertainty on our minds so that we consider each day whether the relationship of ourselves to Christ is such that a welcome in the house of the Father is assured.

The other day I mentioned this concern to a woman who was very negligent in her use of the means of grace. She answered by praising the God-fearing parents who had pointed her to God. I asked if her children would follow her with the same praise after her departure. Then came a confession. She and a friend had been talking about that same subject. The friend said, "What sometimes worries me is what my children will say about me later in life because I am not sending them to church and Sunday school as my folks sent me." I asked for the name and address of that friend.

A few days later the newspapers flashed the headlines of a plane crash in Bryce Canyon. I scanned the casualty list. How startled I was to read the name of the woman who admitted that she failed to give Christian training to her children. How suddenly she had been called to face not the judgment of those children but the judgment of Almighty God. *Today* for you is still *the day of grace.*

14 Serve Jehovah with Gladness

Bible Reading: Psalm 100

Serve the Lord with gladness! Come into his presence with singing! Ps. 100:2.

An offhand remark made by a parishioner some years ago set me to thinking. She told about a relative who was leading a worldly life. This relative did not believe in a heaven or a hell. "You know," she said, "if I didn't believe in a hereafter, I would go out and have a good time, too." That remark reminded me of what the elder brother said when the prodigal son returned. "You never gave me a kid," he said to his father, "that I might make merry with my friends." Poor fellow! He had an altogether wrong conception of religion. To him it was all work and duty, with none of the radiant joy of which Scripture speaks so often.

Are you serving the Lord with gladness? If you let your children think that Christians are always long-faced and sober, then you should not be surprised if they want nothing to do with Christianity. Christianity is the religion of joy, of singing and of gladness. The world is watching you more than you realize. If they see nothing but black, you may expect that they will not be attracted to come to Christ. "Rejoice in the Lord always; again I will say, Rejoice" (Phil. 4:4). Rejoice when you have your family devotions. Rejoice when on God's Day you go to His house. Rejoice!

15 Remember the Angels

Bible Reading: Psalm 34:1—10

*The angel of the Lord encamps around those
who fear him, and delivers them* Ps. 34:7.

Thank God for the angels.

Every day so many things can happen to us and our
children. As you think about that, do you remember
many times when tragedies were averted by an unseen
hand? I think, for example, of the time our son at the
age of two years was nearly drowned. Another day we
were hurrying along the highway between Los Angeles
and San Diego. Our youngsters were in the back seat
when the back door flew open. Then I recall our text.

Today remember the angels and draw encouragement from and rejoice in the protecting mercy of God
through His angels. Commend yourself and your children to the Lord with a new recognition of the greatness of the divine resources. Recall again Hebrews 1:14
where the author says of the angels, "Are they not all
ministering spirits sent forth to serve, for the sake of
those who are to obtain salvation?"

John Calvin says, "Angels are the dispensers and
administrators of the divine beneficence towards us
. . . they guard our safety, undertake our defense, direct
our ways, and exercise a constant solicitude that no
evil befall us. The declarations belong first to Christ
and then to all the faithful, 'He will give his angels
charge of you to guard you in all your ways. . . . The
angel of the Lord encamps around those who fear him,
and delivers them.' "

16 Today — Hear His Voice

Bible Reading: Psalm 95

O that today you would hearken to his voice! Ps. 95:7.

Are you prepared to listen to God's voice *today*? Yes, you listened yesterday. And you are planning to listen tomorrow or some other future day. But today is the all-important day. Yesterday cannot be recalled; tomorrow does not exist. Today is the only day over which you have control. You live only one day at a time, and that day is today. Today is the only day in which you can make restitution for the mistakes of the past. Today is the only day in which you can build safeguards against the future.

If today is such an extraordinarily significant one for you, it is important that you get your instructions from a reliable source. God speaks to you through His Word. Hear His voice today. He emphasizes the message from His Word by means of your experiences. Hear His voice today.

So important is this brief sentence that God caused it to be placed in the Bible four times. Once in Psalm 95, twice in the third chapter of Hebrews, and once again in the fourth chapter of Hebrews.

Hear His voice today. There may not be a tomorrow.

17 What Really Counts

Bible Reading: Luke 10:38–42

Martha, Martha, you are anxious and troubled about many things; one thing is needful. Mary has chosen the good portion, which shall not be taken away from her   Luke 10:41, 42.

Most of us have many important things we feel must be done. We are frightfully busy—with very legitimate interests, with things that it would be sinful to neglect!

But however busy we may be, we should not get lost in details. It is easy to overdo secondary things, even in our service for the Lord!

There is a place in our Christian service for all types of religious activity. And no one activity must crowd out the other. There is room for the activist as well as for the meditative type. Often we tend to think that the kind of service we are rendering the Lord is the only worthy kind. Like Martha and Mary, each of us thinks the other ought to be doing what she is doing.

There is a scale of values. Always the need of the soul must come first. We can be so busy bringing in the kingdom that we neglect to let it grow in our own hearts. Whatever we do, we must not neglect the personal spiritual interests of our lives.

Martha and Mary were both busy, serving the Lord. But Mary *also* "sat at the Lord's feet and listened to his teaching." Whatever our service, or our work, if we are too busy for that, then we are *too busy.*

18 Worthy Praise

Bible Reading: Proverbs 31:10– 31

A woman who fears the Lord is to be praised   Prov. 31:30.

The world's conception of a praiseworthy woman is often a very superficial one. The one praises outward grace and beauty. It lavishes attention on the winners of beauty contests, the stars of the theater and television, and on women who have a place in public life.

The type of woman God honors has a deeper characteristic — she is a woman who fears the Lord. The woman who loves the Lord is marked by Christian love and tenderness. She is a blessing to her husband and children.

The God-fearing woman shall be praised. "Her husband rises up, and he praises her: Many women have done excellently, but you surpass them all" (vs. 28). This is the familiar language of true love. The praise of love is common with young people in courtship. But it is made more precious when deepened and mellowed with the years. It is a blessing when after years of married life a husband says, "There are many fine women in the world, but you are the best of them all." Luther once said, "A man's greatest gift of God is a pious, amiable spouse who fears God, loves His house, and with whom he can live in perfect confidence."

A godly woman is also praised by her children. "Her children rise up and call her blessed." In these days of unhappy and broken homes, pray for and praise our God-fearing wives and mothers.

19 Linked Lives

Bible Reading: 2 Timothy 1:1– 7

. . . I am reminded of your sincere faith, a faith that dwelt first in your grandmother Lois and your mother Eunice and now, I am sure, dwells in you   2 Tim. 1:5.

Lois, Eunice, Timothy. Grandmother, Mother, Son. Three generations linked together. Their lives were linked together by physical generation in natural life, but they were also linked together by regeneration and faith in spiritual life. That is a graphic illustration of what we are accustomed to call God's covenant with us.

Our homes are so very important in the training of children in the faith. Within the intimate and loving framework of the family circle there can be a bequest of spiritual experience and life, passed on in love from the older to the younger.

How important is the spiritual climate that prevails in the home! Real interest in the Scriptures, sincere prayer, genuine Christian conversation, hymns echoing through the rooms, these and many more things help create an atmosphere in which unfeigned faith is nourished and grows. Each generation will possess the same faith, and yet it will not be the same. Each will have its own stamp.

What a responsibility parents have for impressionable children, with whom their lives are linked! Someone tells of two little children who stamped their footprints in a freshly paved street. Two days later when an animal parade passed that way, the elephants left not a single impression. Fifty pounds of boy can do more on a soft pavement than a ton of elephants when it hardens. And children's minds and hearts are also impressionable when they are young.

20 Remember the Sabbath Day

Bible Reading: Deuteronomy 5:12–15

Remember the sabbath day, to keep it holy Exod. 20:8.

Going! Going! Almost gone! What's almost gone? *The traditional Lord's Day as a day of Christian worship.* You have heard an auctioneer shout: "Going once! Going twice! Sold!" Something like that rings in our ears when we watch what is happening to Sunday in America. There are alarming evidences that the old-fashioned Sunday, when the above text was taken to heart by many people in our land, is vanishing.

Sunday sports, radio and TV spectaculars, crowded resort areas, have pretty well eclipsed the observance of the Lord's Day when families were together at both worship services enjoying family fellowship that centered in the home and the church. No, we cannot turn time back, nor should we promote a straitjacket-mentality with respect to things that can be properly enjoyed on Sunday. But what we are witnessing today threatens to blow away everything precious to the believer who takes God's commandment seriously.

It is important that parents recognize the sin and peril of this whole business. Many of the assaults against Sunday are slanted particularly in the direction of youth. The greedy and ungodly barons of commercialized amusements are gunning for our boys and girls. These children are the adults of tomorrow, and unchristian industries are out to get their patronage and support. Encourage your children and young people to honor their Lord by taking a positive stand against all forms of Sunday desecration.

21 But They Returned Home Again

Bible Reading: Acts 21:1—6

And they all, with wives and children, brought us on our way till we were outside the city; and kneeling down on the beach we prayed and bade one another farewell. Then we went on board the ship, and they returned home Acts 21:5, 6.

A group of Christian friends accompanied Paul to the ship. There were children in that small band. What an impression this incident must have made on them! The curtain was quickly drawn on the scene. "Then we went on board the ship, and they returned home." Paul, accompanied by his companions, was on his way to Rome. He never returned. Paul's friends returned to their homes and only the memory of the event remained.

Having witnessed the parting farewells was a priceless experience to these children. Later, Paul wrote a letter to the Ephesian church. The children, now grown to young manhood and young womanhood, could say, "I remember Paul." Who knows how many young people this dauntless missionary recruited for Christ's service by the force of his life? The mental picture of the group kneeling down on the beach could not be erased. Who knows how many of those children irresistibly fell on their knees in later life when they faced the Red Sea of danger and separation?

Memories are so precious and so impressive!

The greatest legacy parents can leave their children is the memory of a Christ-like life.

22 Declare Your Ways to God

Bible Reading: Psalm 119:25–32

When I told of my ways, thou didst answer me Ps. 119:26a.

The hurry of life is so great that it is difficult to sit down quietly for a few moments and tell the Lord about our activities and plans. Still, this could be a rich blessing for you, whether you tell Him about past experiences or about future plans. The Bible states: Declare your ways to God. Confess to Him your ways in the quiet evening hour before night descends. Confess them on your knees. Tell them one by one, and especially do not forget the sinful ways in which you wandered away from God. Yes, confess these first with tears of repentance. He listens to the story of all your ways. And only His listening makes things better.

But when He listens, He also answers. He feels that your telling Him all your ways is not only a matter of thanksgiving, but also a prayer for pardon.

Tell Him about your plans for the future, for today, and for tomorrow. Tell Him about the measures you are taking to bring joy and prosperity to your home. Tell Him these plans on your knees. You must bring them to God before you execute them. Then your ways pass His scrutiny before you begin to follow them. Perhaps He eliminates some plans because they might lead you astray, and on others He pours His indispensable blessing.

23 Fearfully and Wonderfully Made

Bible Reading: Psalm 139

I will praise thee; for I am fearfully and wonderfully made; . . . and that my soul knoweth right well   Ps. 139:14 (*KJV*).

A baby born into a home is a great gift of God. Although father and mother are both intimately involved, the fact remains that the baby is a gift of God fearfully and wonderfully made. The presence of all necessary body functions, the presence of all the essential factors needed for normal growth, the presence of a mind and soul that will come to maturity through the years as the body itself also develops, all speak of that which is utterly beyond the scope of mere human provision. Some people may be willing to settle for mere cause and effect and give no further thought to the miracle involved. But that is a surrender of mind and a stupid refusal to ask the appropriate question: What lies behind such wonderful gathering together of pulsing forces that makes possible such living, throbbing activity that we with eager hands pick up to cuddle?

God says in this psalm: "I am the maker, and when it comes to the deepest mysteries of life, it is I who makes it real; and when it comes to the lifespan that shall be completed, I know the end from the beginning."

What an amazing disclosure. No one is simply part of mass humanity. Every human being is known to God individually. Each is a someone known to Him. Jesus speaks of the sparrows on the housetop as being under God's care and then gives the assurance: "You are of more value than many sparrows."

24 More Blessed to Give

Bible Reading: Acts 20:28–35

. . . Remembering the words of the Lord Jesus, how he said, It is more blessed to give than to receive Acts 20:35.

A woman whose garden annually overflowed into the houses of all her neighbors said, "It is give or die." If one shares the fragrance and beauty of the flowers with others, then the garden will increase in beauty and loveliness.

Many of the pleasures and blessings we receive from God, who is the Giver of all blessings, may be shared with others and become a double blessing. There are many ways of giving double service. A wise lady gave some good advice when she said, "Set your candle before the mirror. Don't you know that you get almost the light of two candles that way?" Her suggestion was put into practice by a poor sewing woman who had very little of this world's goods and seldom anything to brighten her dark little home. So whenever someone gave her a flower, she put it in front of a mirror and it seemed that she had two flowers to enjoy.

The old country preacher was telling about the great blessing he received from giving his tithe to the Lord's work. He said that the more he gave to the Lord, the more the Lord would give to him. He said the more he shoveled out, the more the Lord shoveled in, and the Lord had the biggest shovel.

Truly it is more blessed to give than to receive, yet so many people are missing one of the greatest joys of life.

25 The God of All Comfort

Bible Reading: 2 Corinthians 1:3–11

Blessed be the God and Father of our Lord Jesus Christ, the Father of mercies and God of all comfort, who comforts us in all our affliction 2 Cor. 1:3–4.

Last week we buried two Navajo children. Both were about a year old; both died of similar causes. One however was a covenant child, the child of a believing mother. The other was a child of pagan parents. Both mothers loved their babies and wept for them. The Christian mother however had a serene and joyful face in spite of her tears. The other mother did not. Hers was a look of grim resignation such as we often see among the Navajo.

The non-Christian mother carefully gathered all the clothes, toys, dishes, cradle-board, in fact, everything that had been used by the baby, and fearfully burned them, not so much with the idea of removing all reminders of her baby, but to avoid contamination from the child's departed spirit which might return and bring evil.

The Christian mother took the same kind of items back to her home to be used again. She had learned the Christian way. She knew her child belonged to the Lord and that He had taken her to heaven. She thinks of her child's spirit as being safe in the mansions above, where she herself hopes to go some day. She knows the God of all comfort. What a difference that makes!

26 A Child of Prayer

Bible Reading: 1 Samuel 1:21–28

For this child I prayed; and the Lord has granted me my petition which I made to him. Therefore I have lent him to the Lord; as long as he lives, he is lent to the Lord
1 Sam. 1:27–28.

Hannah prayed that she might have a child and she received Samuel as a remarkable answer to prayer. Her joy in answered prayer prompted her to give her child to Jehovah.

The glory of a woman lies in motherhood. It may indeed be considered her supreme calling. The home is the sphere of her power for there she exerts her greatest influence. It is especially a mother's privilege to train and rear sons and daughters for responsible positions in the world. Through her illustrious children she rules the world. Someone has said, "Before God made a great man He first made a great mother." God-fearing mothers make the greatest contributions to humanity. Hannah gave Samuel, a prophet and ruler in Israel.

Because her child was received as a gift from God, she dedicated him to the Lord. He was a covenant child who had the promises and therefore the believing mother had every reason to believe that Samuel was God's own. Had she not prayed for him and received him from the Lord? She surrendered the lad to Jehovah and Samuel served God all the days of his life.

No parent should do less than Hannah did. Only when children are dedicated to the Lord and trained for His service can Christian parents believe that they have discharged their blessed and sacred duty.

27 Training the Child

Bible Reading: Proverbs 22:1–6

Train up a child in the way he should go, and when he is old he will not depart from it Prov. 22:6.

This familiar verse should be burned into the soul of every parent. It is an admonition of extreme importance.

True parents are conscious of the fact that every moment they are with their children they are training them for life. They train by example, character, and life, as well as by the words they speak. Casual, incidental, unguarded words, and expressions leave as deep and abiding an impression as words deliberately intended to influence a child. Parents cannot hope to exert an influence on a child which is higher and better than their own character. Your children will be able to penetrate your disguise. They will know you as you are. They will follow your real example. It will be impossible to hide your real and true self, beliefs, and convictions. Child training must begin with self-training.

Train up a child in the way he should go, that is, in every respect: in habits of daily prayer; in church attendance each Sunday; in Scripture reading and study; in faithful stewardship and giving; in obedience, respect and courtesy; in purity of mind and body.

Train the *child* when he is still a child. Then the task is relatively easy. Delay, and your training will be difficult, inefficient, and done with sorrow and tears.

If you are faithful, here is God's precious promise: "When he is old he will not depart from it."

28 A Storehouse of Spiritual Food

Bible Reading: Colossians 3:12–17

Let the word of Christ dwell in you richly, as you teach and admonish one another in all wisdom. . . . Col. 3:16a.

Can you imagine a baker beginning his day with empty shelves? Can you imagine a popcorn vendor heading for the grandstands with an empty tray? Can you imagine a professor teaching a class without any preparation? Can you imagine a mother attempting to bring God's Word to her child when she has not studied that Word for herself?

Moses wrote: "And these words which I command you this day shall be upon your heart; and you shall teach them diligently to your children. . . ." (Deut. 6:6–7a). We usually emphasize the importance of teaching God's Word to our children, but let us not overlook the prior point! God's Word must, first of all, "be upon our hearts." Paul writes that the Word of Christ should "dwell in you richly."

We thank God for pastors, Church-school teachers, Christian-school teachers, and others who assist in nurturing our children in the Lord. But, parents, God asks us to so immerse ourselves in the Word, that our ministry in the home will be the foundation for our children's growth. It is not enough to send our children *away* for Christian training!

Scripture states very clearly the importance of Christian parents being filled with God's Word, so that they can pass it on generously and meaningfully to their children. May God make us hungry for His Word. Then, from the abundance of what our Father teaches us, may we faithfully share the Good News with our children.

29 He Blessed

Bible Reading: Matthew 14:13–21

And taking the five loaves and the two fish he looked up to heaven, and blessed, and broke and gave the loaves to the disciples
Matt. 14:19.

A criminal-court judge in all seriousness once said, "If all families had prayers, I wouldn't have much to do." Prayer's power is not to be slighted. Before Jesus broke the five loaves, He "blessed." For Him this was not a wooden formality, a superstition, or a magic power, but an expression of *need.*

Family prayers may well be called "God's minutes." The pause for prayer before and after meals need not be long, but it is exceedingly important. Too often children rushing off to school or father's attendance at a meeting interrupt that brief appointment with God. Family prayers and Scripture reading, when done out of faith not only foster a new sense of spiritual unity and strength, but they also provide a spiritual power for the day's activity. The family altar should remain active as a testimony to faith in and dependence on God. Thereby we acknowledge our Father in heaven as the major and sovereign partner in life.

How sad it is that America is slowly discarding family worship! Many parents who were reared in homes where prayers were always offered at the table have abandoned this spiritual vitamin only to find their children adopting a careless and indifferent attitude toward God and the Church. If Jesus asked a blessing on the loaves, how much more does it become us to humbly bow our heads! We cannot live on bread alone. We need God.

30 Quiet Please!

Bible Reading: Psalm 46:1–11

Be still and know that I am God Ps. 46:10.

In recent years, we've become very conscious of pollution and our environment. We now know that chemicals pollute our streams, many times harming fish and wildlife in and along those streams. We find that many of our manufacturing plants pollute the air by belching huge volumes of smoke and chemicals into the atmosphere.

We must also be concerned about noise pollution. Managers of manufacturing plants are becoming increasingly aware of the toll exacted of employees subjected to the noisy clacking of machinery day in, day out. Psychologists indicate that when we're bombarded by noisy sounds, it takes its toll on our entire personality.

When you take your next vacation, spend some time in quiet seclusion. As you relax by your campfire at night, listen not only to the crackling logs, but also the chorus of chirping crickets, and try to enjoy the beautiful sounds of gurgling mountain streams without the accompaniment of a transistor radio.

Times of quietness can also be spiritually beneficial. The psalmist indicates that it is good for us, periodically, to be stopped in our tracks, to be hushed from our own busy noise, and to simply be still and know that God is God. Quiet times are opportunities for us to become reacquainted with the mighty God who so many times comes in a still, small voice. As you make vacation plans, mother, include some planned quiet time. In that quiet time, allow God to speak to your soul. Be refreshed by His grace.